Smooth

SPHYNX

LIVELY! EXOTIC! SWEET!

ACTIVE! UNUSUAL! STRONG!

ABDO
Publishing Company

Katherine Hengel

Consulting Editor, Diane Craig, M.A./Reading Specialist

Published by ABDO Publishing Company
8000 West 78th Street, Edina, Minnesota 55439.

Copyright © 2010 by Abdo Consulting Group, Inc.
International copyrights reserved in all countries.

Printed in the United States.

 PRINTED ON RECYCLED PAPER

Editor: Liz Salzmann
Content Developer: Nancy Tuminelly
Cover and Interior Design and Production:
    Anders Hanson, Mighty Media
Illustrations: Bob Doucet
Photo Credits: Shutterstock

Library of Congress Cataloging-in-Publication Data
Hengel, Katherine.
  Smooth sphynx / Katherine Hengel ; illustrations by Bob
Doucet.
    p. cm. -- (Cat craze)
  ISBN 978-1-60453-726-0
  1. Sphynx cat--Juvenile literature. I. Doucet, Bob, ill. II.
Title.
  SF449.S68H46 2010
  636.8--dc22
                        2009008169

Super SandCastle™ books are created by a team of
professional educators, reading specialists, and content
developers around five essential components—phonemic
awareness, phonics, vocabulary, text comprehension, and
fluency—to assist young readers as they develop reading
skills and strategies and increase their general
knowledge. All books are written, reviewed, and leveled
for guided reading, early reading intervention, and
Accelerated Reader® programs for use in shared, guided,
and independent reading and writing activities to support
a balanced approach to literacy instruction.

CONTENTS

The Sphynx	3
Facial Features	4
Body Basics	5
Coat & Color	6
Health & Care	8
Attitude & Behavior	10
Litters & Kittens	12
Buying a Sphynx	14
Living with a Sphynx	18
The Great Sphynx	20
Find the Sphynx	22
The Sphynx Quiz	23
Glossary	24

The
SPHYNX

The sphynx is an unusual and popular cat. It looks hairless! But actually, a sphynx has short, fine hair called down. This down feels like a warm, fuzzy peach! The sphynx is very active and has large eyes and ears. There are often waiting lists to adopt them.

FACIAL FEATURES

Head

The sphynx has a triangular head. The head is a little bit longer than it is wide.

Muzzle

The sphynx's **muzzle** sticks almost straight out from its face.

Eyes

The sphynx's eyes are large. They are **slanted** and set far apart.

Ears

The sphynx has huge ears! They are wide at the base and point up towards the sky.

BODY
BASICS

Size

Adult sphynx weigh about 8 to 10 pounds (4 to 5 kg).

Build

The sphynx has a long, **slender** body. It is muscular and very strong for its size.

Tail

Sphynx have long, slender tails that come to a point.

Legs and Feet

They have thin, short legs and round paws. They have long toes and thick pads on their paws.

COAT & COLOR

Sphynx Fur

Sphynx are sometimes called hairless cats, but they actually have hair! A fine down covers their **slender** bodies. Some have longer hair on the nose, tail, and toes.

Other cats have enough fur to **absorb** their body oils. Because sphynx don't have much hair, they need to be bathed once a week!

Sphynx usually have wrinkled skin around their **muzzles**, between their ears, and around their shoulders.

SEAL POINTED

Sphynx come in many different colors and patterns.
The photos on these pages show just a few examples.

| BLUE MACKEREL TABBY | TORTOISESHELL | SOLID WHITE |

HEALTH & CARE

Life Span

Sphynx can live for 15 years or longer!

Health Concerns

Sphynx are generally healthy. They should not spend a long time in the sun. Because their skin isn't covered with fur, sphynx can get sunburned. Sphynx can also get cold easily. They are happiest in a **temperate** climate.

8

VET'S CHECKLIST

- Give your sphynx a bath once a week.

- Have your sphynx spayed or neutered. This will prevent unwanted kittens.

- Visit a vet for regular checkups.

- Clean your sphynx cat's teeth and ears once a week.

- Ask your vet about shots that may benefit your cat.

- Ask your vet which foods are right for your sphynx.

ATTITUDE & BEHAVIOR

Personality

Friendly and **loyal**, sphynx like to follow their owners around. Some even wag their tails like dogs! The sphynx is a charming **breed** that loves attention. They are affectionate and social. They usually get along with other cats and dogs.

Activity Level

Sphynx are very lively, active cats! Most sphynx act more like acrobats than cats. They like to jump off of tall objects, such as refrigerators or shelves. They love to amuse their human companions!

All About Me

Hi! My name is Sapphire. I'm a sphynx. I just wanted to let you know a few things about me. I made some lists below of things I like and dislike. Check them out!

Things I Like

- Jumping off of high shelves
- Playing with other cats and dogs
- Staying clean and warm
- Performing tricks
- Playing inside with toys
- Following my owner around the house
- Getting a lot of attention

Things I Dislike

- Being outside in the cold
- Spending a lot of time alone
- Getting really dirty
- Being in small places
- Being outside in the hot sun

LITTERS & KITTENS

Litter Size

Female sphynx usually give birth to two to four kittens.

Diet

Newborn kittens drink their mother's milk. They can begin to eat kitten food when they are about five weeks old. Kitten food is different from cat food. It has extra **protein**, fat, and **vitamins** that help kittens grow.

Growth

Sphynx kittens should stay with their mothers until they are 14 to 15 weeks old. A sphynx will be almost full grown when it is six months old. But it will continue to grow slowly until it is one year old.

BUYING A SPHYNX

Choosing a Breeder

It's best to buy a kitten from a **breeder**, not a pet store. When you visit a cat breeder, ask to see the mother and father of the kittens. Make sure the parents are healthy, friendly, and well behaved.

Picking a Kitten

Choose a kitten that isn't too active or too shy. If you sit down, some of the kittens may come over to you. One of them might be the right one for you!

Is It the Right Cat for You?

Buying a cat is a big decision. You'll want to make sure your new pet suits your lifestyle.

Get out a piece of paper. Draw a line down the middle.

Read the statements listed here. Each time you agree with a statement from the left column, make a mark on the left side of your paper. When you agree with a statement from the right column, make a mark on the right side of your paper.

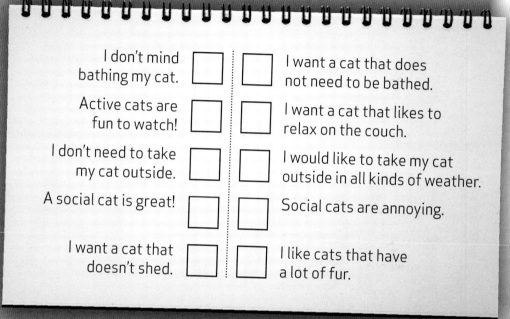

I don't mind bathing my cat.	☐	☐	I want a cat that does not need to be bathed.
Active cats are fun to watch!	☐	☐	I want a cat that likes to relax on the couch.
I don't need to take my cat outside.	☐	☐	I would like to take my cat outside in all kinds of weather.
A social cat is great!	☐	☐	Social cats are annoying.
I want a cat that doesn't shed.	☐	☐	I like cats that have a lot of fur.

If you made more marks on the left side than on the right side, a sphynx may be the right cat for you! If you made more marks on the right side of your paper, you might want to consider another breed.

Some Things You'll Need

Cats go to the bathroom in a **litter box**. It should be kept in a quiet place. Most cats learn to use their litter box all by themselves. You just have to show them where it is! The dirty **litter** should be scooped out every day. The litter should be changed completely every week.

Your cat's **food and water dishes** should be wide and shallow. This helps your cat keep its whiskers clean. The dishes should be in a different area than the litter box. Cats do not like to eat and go to the bathroom in the same area.

Cats love to scratch! **Scratching posts** help keep cats from scratching the furniture. The scratching post should be taller than your cat. It should have a wide, heavy base so it won't tip over.

Cats are natural predators. Without small animals to hunt, cats may become bored and unhappy. **Cat toys** can satisfy your cat's need to chase and capture. They will help keep your cat entertained and happy.

Cats should not play with balls of yarn or string. If they accidentally eat the yarn, they could get sick.

Cat claws should be trimmed regularly with special cat claw **clippers**. Regular nail clippers will also work. Some people choose to have their cat's claws removed by a vet. But most vets and animal rights groups think declawing is cruel.

A **cat bed** will give your cat a safe, comfortable place to sleep.

LIVING WITH A SPHYNX

Being a Good Companion

Sphynx are special cats that need special attention. They need to be bathed once a week. Unlike other cats, a sphynx only takes a few seconds to dry! Also, their large ears need to be cleaned weekly. Sphynx should be trained to **tolerate** these **grooming** practices when they are young.

Inside or Outside?

It's a good idea to keep your sphynx inside. Sphynx do not have much fur to keep them warm or protect their skin. Most vets and **breeders** agree that it is best for cats to be kept inside. That way the cats are safe from predators and cars.

18

Feeding Your Sphynx

Sphynx may be fed regular cat food. Your vet can help you choose the best food for your cat.

Cleaning the Litter Box

Like all cats, sphynx like to be clean. They don't like smelly or dirty litter boxes. If the litter box is dirty, they may go to the bathroom somewhere else. Ask your vet for advice if your cat isn't using its box.

 DANGER: POISONOUS FOODS

Some people like to feed their cats table scraps. Here are some human foods that can make cats sick.

TOMATOES   **POTATOES**

ONIONS   **GARLIC**

CHOCOLATE   **GRAPES**

THE GREAT SPHYNX

Cats with very little fur have existed since the early 1900s. In 1902, a couple from New Mexico received two cats from local Pueblo Indians. Some believed that these cats were the last of an ancient Aztec **breed**. The cats looked a lot like the sphynx that we know today.

The sphynx cat is named after a **mythological** beast called a sphinx. It had a lion's body and a human head.

The most famous sphinx is the Great Sphinx of Giza. This huge sculpture is 65 feet (20 m) tall and 241 feet (74 m) long!

FIND THE SPHYNX

A

B

C

D

THE SPHYNX QUIZ

1. Sphynx have short, fine hair called down. **True or false?**

2. The sphynx has very small ears. **True or false?**

3. Sphynx need to be bathed once a week. **True or false?**

4. Sphynx come in many different colors and patterns. **True or false?**

5. Sphynx can get sunburned. **True or false?**

6. The sphynx does not like attention. **True or false?**

GLOSSARY

absorb – to soak up or take in.

breed – a group of animals or plants with common ancestors. A *breeder* is someone whose job is to breed certain animals or plants.

groom – to clean the fur of an animal.

loyal – faithful or devoted to someone or something.

muzzle – the nose and jaws of an animal.

mythological – having to do with myths.

protein – a substance found in all plant and animal cells.

slanted – not level or straight.

slender – slim or thin.

temperate – having mild temperatures.

tolerate – to allow something to be done.

vitamin – a substance needed for good health, found naturally in plants and meats.

About SUPER SANDCASTLE™

Bigger Books for Emerging Readers
Grades K–4

Created for library, classroom, and at-home use, Super SandCastle™ books support and engage young readers as they develop and build literacy skills and will increase their general knowledge about the world around them. Super SandCastle™ books are part of SandCastle™, the leading preK–3 imprint for emerging and beginning readers. Super SandCastle™ features a larger trim size for more reading fun.

Let Us Know

Super SandCastle™ would like to hear your stories about reading this book. What was your favorite page? Was there something hard that you needed help with? Share the ups and downs of learning to read. We want to hear from you! Send us an e-mail.

sandcastle@abdopublishing.com

Contact us for a complete list of SandCastle™, Super SandCastle™, and other nonfiction and fiction titles from ABDO Publishing Company.

www.abdopublishing.com • 8000 West 78th Street Edina, MN 55439 • 800-800-1312 • 952-831-1632 fax